TALES OF THE AFTERLIFE

by
Gary Beaumier

UnCollected Press

Cover Art:

Photo by Gary Beaumier

Back Cover Portrait:

Photo by Mary Beaumier

Book Design by:

UnCollected Press
8320 Main Street, 2nd Floor
Ellicott City, MD 21043

For more books by UnCollected Press:
www.therawartreview.com

First Edition 2023

ISBN: 979-8-9883022-7-8

Table of Contents

little something for the pain...1

All Too Short a Time..2

The Shape of My Absence...4

Singing Love Songs on Pluto 6

you who presume to know me 7

Spirit Animal...8

Sirocco 10

For All Seasons 11

Hello Icarus 13

The Ukrainian Seamstress 14

Far From Myself...15

In Absentia 17

Wintering 18

Rain in Dublin...19

Moon Goddess...20

An Approximation of Birds 21

Bring Me Devils and Ghosts 22

Small Offerings to the God of Letting Go 23

July 10, 1939...24

The World in Question..26

Render Me Onto 27

Merely Us 29

He Called Me Zelda...30

Panhandler's Lullaby..32

Continental Drift 34

October...35

Tales of the Afterlife.. 36

Midnight at the Antiquarian Book Shop.......................... 38

The Great Continuum.. 40

From Certain Distances In Space I Still See My Brother 43

Only Catholic Boys Remember All Their Sins 44

How She Grieved the Old Piano...................................... 45

The Way Station 46

The Migratory Habits of Dreams in Late Autumn 47

Sunrise Suite for Cello and Piano 48

Future Tense 49

Dmitri I Have No Music for This 52

Here I Sing 54

Places I Have Known... 55

Rain to Snow 57

Re-imagining My Father.. 58

Remembering Your Repeated Attempts at Living............ 60

Some Still Come to Ask... 62

TEN CENTS 63

The Northern Lights.. 64

2 a.m. Charlie.. 66

Found... 67

West With the Night.. 68

Every Single Toe... 69

Gone Askew... 70

Oh Ferdinand... 71

Where We Left Off.. 72

The Forgers.. 73

Night Forest... 75

To Mary, always to my beloved Mary, for her wise counsel, her shrewd editing, her unstinting encouragement, and her tolerance of all my idiosyncratic ways.

To my son and daughter Ben and Mara who are now older and wiser than me. Hang in there. All my love.

little something for the pain

wear many layers of clothes
to pad your falls

watch tv late into a sleepless night
just to shatter the devastating quiet

i've got this poultice for the heart

i know of this analgesic for darker thoughts

a potion for world weariness
a refuge in your bedroom
where the sorry news cannot reach you

place these words beneath your tongue
working their way into your bloodstream
phrases syringed into a usable vein
poems to obliterate the angst and emptiness

this is a word apothecary
a little something for the pain

All Too Short a Time

I think I know a little something of your mind, the landscapes of your
animal soul.

You listen carefully to my words;
maybe to you they are
undulating and musical and rhythmic.

Are there gales in your head sometimes,
waves thrashing
with the cries of gulls and geese?

And in the quiet spring days of our walks do you hear the movement of
trees as they stretch a little more toward the sky?

You find
flowers to be sniffed
along with deer shit and strange dogs' piss.
You know smells like I know words in a book.
All those times I watched you
tilt your nose up to let it follow some ribbon of scent carried on the soft
morning air. New life or decay?
I'll likely never know.

You glory running along the sands with a far
too large stick in your mouth.
That is your moment entirely.

You are a keen student of my moods,
when my thoughts are rain-lashed,
cut by lightning and jarred with the concussions of some inner tempest,
and at those times you won't allow me to be alone.

Every morning I feel the press of your muzzle on my side of the bed
your nose pink like a pencil eraser
as you celebrate my awakening?

Thank you for your unspoiled gladness at my every return,

the furious sweep of your tail, your melting soulful looks.

Thank you for eating my fine Italian leather shoes. We both have refined taste in footwear.

Always let me remember your shorter time here and be with you a little more completely.

Because one day in the car I will say to you,
  This is your last trip, old friend".
and then agonize about whether I shouldn't let your broken body fight a little longer.

The Shape of My Absence

I usually get it wrong in my head
these passages of conversations I hold with you
over my passages across your waters

I want you to know I am always counting backwards

I want you to know I will be a last minute Buddhist
though it may make up for nothing

Be my confessor as I pitch my sins to you
like a child skipping stones

I feel the undertow of melancholy
when your torn clouds have curtained the horizon

and for all my resolve to stay away I am back the next day
though you may break me over your fortifications of rocks

I have marked you for a killer
you will take a child as easily as an old man
you will scatter your birds over your waves
yield your fish to the hook
days when you are tender
mornings of peaked waves and
wind-whipped froth

you have damaged me with your icy cold and I have somehow I adored
you anyway
as I walked into the teeth of your rage
 It's nothing personal" you say
 nothing personal"

you have carried my fat little boat
sweetly along your shores
though I know how easily your temper could change

like the jostling of a lover I have felt the lingering of your pitch and roll long after I have come back to land

one day you will ask for me and I will walk into your sunrise
—a glorious red blooming of clouds—
I will follow my dog there
or he will follow me

and we will be companions again in a different place
and you will be the shape of my absence

Singing Love Songs on Pluto

I once had a house on Pluto
with a wrap around porch
where I would sing love songs
in the permanent night pierced in stars

Later I flew vast tracks of the southern ocean
in my Gypsy Moth
dolphins vaulting over waves
all held in freeze frame
and as my little plane sped along
I tipped my wings in greeting
to the occasional steamer below
and when I landed in your garden
I held myself in stillness
as the world harmonized all around me

You once told me love was nothing but a bribe
meant to fill the empty spaces in ourselves
and so I said to you,
"bribe me anyway"
and then I serenaded you through the night
song after song
which made you laugh and laugh

you who presume to know me

did not know i watched a hermit crab keeping company with a starfish
this morning in a tide pool

or that i peed in a wooded area beyond the salt grass

that i followed the grey silhouette of a freighter northbound and making
heavy weather

that i licked my lips to taste the brine air

that i imagined myself the sole dweller
of a tiny island where i had a stout dory
to row to the coastal village in my yellow slicker
my arthritic hands gripping the oars

you will never know that i talk to the gulls
and they answered me back

or that i nearly wept when i saw a whale breach

or that i watched the rise of the sun that electrified the edges of clouds

that i picked wood violets to lay next to a fallen tern just beyond the
reach of the surf

will they find me some winter's day
frozen and gone and
all my wanderings ceased
the last of my dreams
dreaming a passage back home to you

Spirit Animal

For a dollar I will sing your favorite song.
Do you mind if my voice careens off the notes a bit
and if it quavers?

For five dollars we will sit in your car
in the rain
the motor running
the wipers sweeping
overlooking the city
and you can tell me your stories
and I will refund all your money
if you come back tomorrow
and listen to me.

Then I will tell you if I were a fisherman
I would fish without a hook
just to feel mesmerized by the waves.

And you will say if you were a hunter
you wouldn't put bullets in your gun
and only listen to the way a forest prays.

If we were soldiers
we would shout jokes at the enemy
just to hear them laugh.

You will tell me some part of you is a hummingbird
seeking a little nectar in a half gale.

I will say I am a stray dog
dodging city traffic and living off scraps.

Then the rain will stop and
we will lean against the hood
to share a pull of cheap gin from my flask
while I blow cigarette smoke up toward the fleeing clouds
and you will say,
 at least now we know who we are."

So, I looked for you day after day after that
but you never did return.

Sirocco

Long after the banquet of love I have danced with your afterimage
against a backdrop of sleep and memory
I recall the lingering of your scent
the delicate alchemy of perfume and sweat
I feel the phantom sensations of your flesh and you grind against me
your soft exhalations
like the African wind swept across the Mediterranean over my chest and
belly
We were lion and lioness in mutual conquest escorting one another
to our perfect little deaths

Did these memories wobble and shift like dreams
watery and insubstantial
Did they morph into kind lies
in time's length
or was this real after all
and I only now cherish the moment
so long past

How I wish to return to that place
—to kill you once again—
to surrender everything to you.

For All Seasons

Spring

I float in your secret sea
I feel the buzz of your words
From some slim volume
in my liquid world
not knowing outside
things green and push
through the soil
while frogs orchestrate
such a cacophony of life

Summer

Read me into a bright morning
as we lean against a leaving oak
A book about a toad and badger and rat and mole
while I pluck a blade of grass a ladybug has scaled
as I lean my head into the safety of your warm body
your voice a song to me

Fall

It is a weathered park bench
it is me with a book
maybe I have as many days left
as those I've spent
leaves rustle in the wind like an up ended biography
I sit alone
with the best of companions

Winter

Spin me a tale of places and things unknown
since I am soon to take a slow train there
across fields of deepening snow swirled into drifts
frost etchings on the window as we pass electric blue lakes
and then into forests of scarce daylight

while my eyes dim and my breathing shallows
and my grip has let go of all my worldly things
then read me the passage that says it all meant something

Hello Icarus

Once I shuffled along the wings of biplanes
I know this because I always fall in my dreams
from very high and unsurvivable places
tugged inexorably toward cliffs
by some invisible force or
tumbling off high buildings

When I get old and rickety
like those planes
I'll take one burst of wind too many
and collapse mid flight impossibly high
guy wires slackened
trailing struts or tail fins as they are loosed
spinning rapidly toward a thicket of trees

Maybe my last words will be "Hello Icarus
I should have known I could only stay aloft so long"
and all the wing walkers said the same
but wasn't it nice to have escaped the pull of gravity
those many times
and finally when the pilot cuts the engine
we drifted down through a soundless world
by the grace of the wings
in that rarified place
only we knew

The Ukrainian Seamstress

A soldier brings his torn field jacket
to her
  So much blown to pieces," he says.
She carries the heavy scent of tobacco
and you can almost see the charred buildings in her eyes like
gravestones.

  There's always someone who wants to break the world, "she answers.

She leads him to her bed again
where he can take her to the forgetting places
and he strokes her hair
and his lips trespass all along her breasts
as he claims her for his inviolate country.

And later when they share a cigarette
—even as a bomb falls nearby
and even as he startles—
she makes him promise to come back to her
even if he is lying.

Then she grieves for everyone this war has smashed
—the ones she knows and the ones she doesn't—
because you cannot stitch them back together
while she traces a finger along a ridge of muscle on his bare shoulder
and whispers a protective mantra for him.

Finally after he leaves
she pushes her face in the torn bedclothes
and inhales his memory
even as she hears the distant crack of a rifle
even as she prays the bullet did not find him.

Far From Myself

I am diluted this morning in my cup of coffee

I am staggered from a dream where
I was a radioactive curiosity
in the middle of a gathering
where I spoke in anachronisms
to puzzled looks.

I have time travelled on the notes of an old tune
and found myself to be someone else.

I am a refugee from a family of lambs:
a little of my father,
more my mother.

I've acquired such inertia
yet I've run long miles
for reasons I've yet to fathom
following others who didn't know either.

I am lost between the lines;
lost in the flecks of brown in your eyes,
between the flecks of brown
a pinwheel of light from a galaxy
tugs me out of myself
and across that vastness.
Was there *another* unrealized
who I should have been
that you should have known?.

Sometimes I scan the old yellowed photos.
How could I not cauterize the seepage of hard memory
with bad whiskey?
Still the demons come.

How do I reclaim myself so late in the day?
The ungodly hours have befriended me
in the comfort of their darkness.

It is there I visit the hill I died on
and wonder if it was worth it.

And then I wonder how I've become
only distantly related to myself.

In Absentia

know me as the unclean
ring the bell
ring the bell

look for me on the off ramps
i will hold a sign that says
  we are much the same"

know my soul delivered to your doorstep
lies between the front cover and the back

if you like
use it to shore up a wobbly table
and give it nothing but your cold eye

know this voice to choke on words

know me as the shadow
that passes between you and your sun

know that embedded in every gesture
every struggle
some crescendo of hope may rise above it
just to be known

and then know the cruelty of hope

someday i will inherit the sun
and paint the clouds
and set the moon upon my lap

one day you look again and see me
and I will be nothing but words
one day you may know me

Wintering

I wonder if you knew when you let the dog out
as the shadows of that late October day crept longer
and there was music playing
—a violin weaving in and out of the gloaming from somewhere—
and he ran to me with joyful abandon as dogs so perfectly do
and there was this scent of burning leaves like something from a church
I wonder if you knew I could have ridden the swift parade of clouds
like islands migrating eastward

but you wore this smile
that made me think you did know this moment like I knew it
and that made me toss my heart to you

and it was all so complete

so glance back upon this
when the snow and darkness close us in
and maybe know it again once or twice
through the long nights of our winter

Rain in Dublin

I want to know what happened to the 90 year old man
who raced up the steps of the Empire State Building several years ago
Has he slipped away in the night in some unremarkable way
while I turned in my sleep

and WH Auden
when his body quit
when he knew of the world's indifference
was I scraping off the evening dinner plates into the garbage

and you mother
at some disconnected hour
in the morning
with your son escorting you
to your very last exhalation
and me your other son between gulps of coffee
not knowing
when I should have been there too

good bye then
as the traffic light changes
and the dogs are let out
good bye

fare thee well
while the geese exchange their places in flight
and the corn grows another inch

adieu
as you sit for your noon day lunch break
watching a fierce blizzard whiten the world
and trading gossip with your colleagues

or is it enough to know that it is raining in Dublin
and to put myself there
a forgiving rain to wash clean my thoughts
as I stumble from a pub
a sad ballad playing in my head

Moon Goddess

I have flown my chromed up Harley
lured straight into a bittersweet moon
that sat at the end of a country lane
engine popping
bathed in thick summer air
my heart smashed from rejected love
so close to meeting James Dean
but this is living too I thought
and so I stayed

I have listened to the slow clang of bells for ancient friends
and felt a pang of envy that the moon goddess took them
but if you find me in the morning
mouth gaped
eyes looking past this world
know that I was seduced
know that I asked her to take me this way
know this body just quit
as they all do
as your dog passes on
and the geranium dies on your porch at the end of the season

She will offer me her porcelain hand
—this moon goddess—
and I will be lifted away
like smoke carried on a breeze off a campfire
to my dispersal
into the rushing clouds of
daybreak

An Approximation of Birds

all my life there have been birds

i cannot sleep because they chatter outside my window

all my life they've come to disrupt

to exploit my empty places

to quicken my heart now
in unseemly ways

and i have wished those birds away
that i may have my dreams back
only to long for them when they are gone

my mind flutters and dizzies
in their confusions of flight
all through the darkness

they think i look ridiculous and they are right to think so
i keep looking for a place where there are no birds
yet they seem to be everywhere

i confess i have loved a few
the ones with the yellow and red plumage
and the ones with the sweet songs
the black ones who seem to mock me
and all of them exact such a price

i have followed the lineage of these loves
all down through my years
their paths through the firmament of my thoughts and memories
their paths through the containment areas of my heart

i am lost amongst them
and i think i may need to find myself one more time
if only i can
because so many birds have changed me

Bring Me Devils and Ghosts

Have I loved the night
for all the wrong reasons?
The sun does me no favors.
But darkness meets my mood
when it carries the indifferent moon
and cold stars prick its black.
Can they be colder than some I've known?

Wrest me from my sleep then
and bring me devils and ghosts
I will raise a glass to them
and be amongst them soon
to be married to the night

Small Offerings to the God of Letting Go

The god of letting go is a volcano.
Give it the rock lodged near your heart.

The god of letting go
is October
all the trees unleaving.

This god has sent you to lower places
and made you ordinary.

He is the night sky.
Send him your grievances.

He is the ocean
where flotillas of paper boats sail
that were once broken hearts.

Assign to each scudding of clouds
on this windy day all you want to be forgiven for
with each gust
another transgression gone
into the great letting go.

But the god of letting go is gone today
or he has had his fill of me
or has been crushed under
an avalanche of woes.

 The god of letting go has written his epitaph
 It was all too much," he said.

July 10, 1939
(On my parents 80th wedding anniversary)

This is a day set in the amber of memory
...the day that set everything in motion

neither could see the coming war
he only saw the white veil
of this 23 year old he'd take

they did not imagine the four
—a girl and the three boys—
evenly spaced until the last

she only saw his blue eyes behind the glasses
the thickness of his oiled hair

they only heard the old priest
in the bright vestments
who prompted their soft replies
with the candle scent of beeswax
in the church's acoustics
that seemed to swallow their words

she only saw his gleaming car
that would take them to Yellowstone
he only felt their awkwardness
and pretended it was normal
as he loaded their luggage in the trunk

there were no strokes or heart failures
or joblessness that darkened the house yet
only this scatter of days
in relief against the tapestry of their futures

so when the car radio lost all the signals
he sang *Alouetta* in the French of French Canadians
and she laughed at the funny sounding words
and she slid across the car seat into his gathering arm
as he glanced at her he could see the flecks of light in her green eyes

24

and later maybe there was hope in the flecks of light in
the night sky as they leaned against the car
in the motel parking lot
even as she felt irrevocably far from home

and she gripped his arm and said, "sing
Red River Valley,"
his sweet baritone notes enfolding her
her eyes with such promise

The World in Question

In a thousand worlds like this did not the rivers run a different course?

In another world did clouds become mountains and the winds offer sweet blessings?

In one of those worlds several moons tugged us out of ourselves to love a little better.

In another place the child was not strafed with murderous words
and the menace in the corners of a mother's mouth softened to a smile.

There is a world where we want less and take joy in what we have,
a country with one less broken soul.

So give the world a different name if we are too fixed to see other places.

But let us not curse the sun
and spit upon the ground on which we stand and instead ask
  Why not?"
and maybe find it perfect in a way that escapes our knowing
and then go to meet it there.

Render Me Onto

When I am turned to ash
sprinkle me on the
back of a cormorant
that I make migrate to a warmer clime

Shake me salty
on robins' eggs
blue as the sky
and see me come spring

Sift my grit between your fingers
and toss me skyward
into a gust of south wind

Dust me on each corner of
our home that I may stay with
you a little longer

As for my recalcitrant parts
the ones you found so difficult in me
give them to the sea
and task it with my softening
to take as an apology
for my living days

Rub a little on the back
of your brown horse
brown as your eyes
so we may ride
a trail to no particular place

Spread a little of me in the paddock

fence posts crooked
from winter's heaving

Take care that the breeze
doesn't toss me back
to flour
your face like a baker
lingering like a kiss there

Merely Us

Under a dark bloom of cumulus
Dense concentrations of geese wander the sky
I have not been listening
I have not listened,
trading all for a sugar high

There is the shushing of the ice
the waves bring to shore
and the sinewy wisps of steam
that skim the waters in the harbor
just before a west wind takes them
near the burning of the sun

There is the watch of the trees
in their slow deliberateness,
in this season of long nights

It is not the world that ends in fire or ice
merely us

He Called Me Zelda

Late Fall winds blow sinister.
I will dress unfashionably,
mummified in layers,
and take my coffee in the little shop.
To those who regard me at all
I'll return a scorching look.
I produce a well thumbed
novel from my pocket
and pretend to read
while the pain in my hip pulses.

What should I wear today?
An old dress from another era
as snow threatens.
I will fall asleep in the chair by the window,
and find myself cloaked in twilight,
my cup gone cold.
I will not have spoken a word to anyone all the day
as I hear the church bell
and ask myself "is this a Monday?"

I am dressed in wrinkles
and wear pouches under my eyes.
My feet are always cold
and I wonder if I wear the scent
of mothballs and decay.

Should I hasten the inevitable?
Do I leave a note?…
To whom it may concern
I will locate the femoral artery
Do it quickly
Don't think
Just one slash

I will fortify myself with the cognac I drank in Paris
all those years ago.
I feel a spasm of memory

as I recall a boy I loved who called me Zelda

and I called him Scott
and we pretended to be Jazz Age hipsters.
Even in our boozy dissipation I felt redeemed.

I wish I knew what happened to that boy
but if I could find him again in my next life
I'd leave right now.

Panhandler's Lullaby

look away as you glide down the off ramp
pulse the door locks
pray the light to green
or turn up your Brahms

do not glimpse his brief prayer
on tattered cardboard
his three word biography

he will shelter in a vacant doorway this night
mistaken for a pile of rags
suckling on some cheap booze
that will burn a path down his esophagus
while a cutting wind scampers litter past him

yet was he not celebrated at birth
by a mother who sang him back to sleep
after he took from her given breast

there will be thumping music at 3 am
that breaks into his unconsciousness
and at some point in the night
the bladder will not hold
and he will shiver and sing out for his mother

come the next evening he will find the old
busker near the underpass by the tent city
and he will blot the dribbled whisky from the scraggle of his beard
on the back of his sleeve as he wheezes out a cough
and then he will rise unsteadily to toss a few crumpled bills into the
music case
and listen to the trumpet measure sweet notes that echo and drift off of
the concrete

"Play Taps" he will tell the horn player

and his memory will drift back to the war when he watched the soldier
ahead of him
step on a land mine

32

his body shredded into a pink mist

and he will choose to remember that soldier
even as he wishes to forget

Continental Drift

we were once a single land mass
you and I
earth and rock fused together by Vulcan himself
nary a line between us

then came little fissures of resentment
anger cracked the surface
and though still within reach
our masses separated and cold drafts swept the chasm in our bedrock

the said and unsaid inched us away
even as we reached across the distance sometime
but no more to explore the terrain

still I love you South America
your gay cities
your jungles
your mountain peaks

and you still regard me with a glint in your eye
my heat and squalor and brooding darkness

and I have missed your shape once pressed into my western shores

October

In the season of old
October squanders so much light

All these wishes made foolish
now that we have crested the place they call *aged*

In the end night pries our grip from everything we know

My feet shuffle through a rain soaked congestion of leaves
as darkness works it sleight of hand

Walk with me a little then my love
I am hobbled
clutch my sleeve I am wrinkled
kiss my cheek

all our memories limp behind

Tales of the Afterlife

Monday morning broods into a muted gray while
sleeplessness churns the mind
to the raw and incomplete.

The city air is scented with the exhaust of automobiles
and congested with the offense of their noise.

I slip on the ice and curse.
Maybe I should have just gone with the fall
body limp as a rag doll.

Years back snow geese died in mid flight
spiraling down
              down
                   down
I will learn their path
should I go in mid sentence
after some conspiracy of the vessels in my brain
or some burst of my heart
to cease on the most ordinary of days.

And to those who tell tales of the afterlife
I will wake to the morning
pushed into the world through my mother
to stand on spindly legs

or break through the soil
to engage the sun
in hopes of a far reach into the sky

crack through a shell
and come to ride currents of air
above a thickness of clouds

swim amongst the corals
in a world of dazzling color

howl in the night in concert with man's sirens

We are not so separate as we suppose

and the wind will carry me again and again
into still another being
and through another night
just as it always has.

Midnight at the Antiquarian Book Shop

"I was most grievously undone
when I lost my footing on the shelf
and swan dived to the floor
splayed and back broken,"
says *The Complete Works of Shakespeare*
who now leans against the cash register

"We are— so many of us— a musty assemblage of forgotten words.
Trees pressed into paper to hold our messages.
Conceived by some dreamy word dabbler long gone.
Escorting the appreciative few from womb to tomb
Yet now shorn of dust jacket
now a deterioration of spine
dog eared pages and torn scripts
Are we soon to be consigned to a burn pile?"

The Selected Poems of Elizabeth Barret Browning flutters her pages
"Slings and arrows, Will," she says woefully,
"slings and arrows"

"One for all" rallies
a volume of the stories of Dumas

"Ours is not to reason why" says Tennyson on the third shelf in 19th
century literature

"Still the bespectacled girl comes by after school
And slips a kind hand around me"
asserts a copy of *Wind in the Willows*
"Loses herself in my illustrations, she does.
Toad and Badger still wing her imagination."

"I'm hitting the road" says a copy of Kerouac's complete works.

"Where you going to go, Jack?" asks Alan Ginsburg caressing his cover
lovingly.

"The doors are all locked."

An old dog escapes from Herriot's work
and nuzzles the bard.

"Read to us William
in your stentorian voice."
they all plead
"Read us through the night.
We still love you."

…and so he begins *A Midsummer Night's Dream*
while the other volumes nod approvingly.

The Great Continuum

I mistook you for the angry sunrise this morning putting fire to the clouds

I knew the furious waves were not you
stumbling towards the beach, were they?

What funny turns my grieving takes these days.

Someone said the gull cried out in your voice but I'm sure they were mistaken.

Didn't you spend all your days trying not to be one of them?

And yet when the worms have had their way
what will we become
if not a fish
if not a flower?

I once was a full moon lighting borders
I knew imagination was forbidden to cross.

I am now gnarled as an old tree
praying for the center to hold
I may soon become a laughing child
consorting with the wind
kicking over headstones
and toppling monuments.

Rain

This house is worn
and comfortable and I know
its music
the furnace igniting
the sigh of the wind in the gable
the snare drum rattle of window pane
it is an old friend as I listen to
the hush of a brother's breathing near

Down the hall
the conversational
patter of my mother
and dad as they bed
for the night
and the sounds
of when they take to each other
like a much needed rain

Years since when
my life parched
I've stolen a late evenings
walk past that house
we still know each other
that place and I
as I search through
windows for memories kept
—the world and sky about to break—
and I think
you were much needed rain

and down the lane
where they have bedded
in the ground
—mother and father—
no more whisperings

in the night
as I stand over them
simply to abide my longing

From Certain Distances In Space I Still See My Brother

Somewhere mother holds you against her breasts in a Chicago flat
-- the war winding down --
while she warms a bottle and tests the milk on the tender of her wrist;
"you are my sunshine," she sings.

Somewhere you sit in a quilted coat
upon a tricycle in front of a red house,
and later still your fastball hisses over
home plate into the strike zone.

Somewhere a man says we all derive from stars,
while a holy person declares we will live forever.

You still succor your fractious babies as you pace a midnight floor.

Only just now a distant planet watches you bend to help a student
or soften your embrace to your wife in the utter dark.

Somehow you glide out of a fifth floor hospital room into a painted
twilight,
into streams of cars and trucks and exhaust
as your family holds your emancipated body and rides with you to the
edge of life

and somewhere a medical student
peels back what remains of you
to learn the human clockwork.

Only Catholic Boys Remember All Their Sins

Joseph ate french fries before taking the Eucharist when he should have fasted

Thomas stole a Hershey Bar from the Five and Dime while the clerk was in the backroom and then vomited it up on purpose to make up for his theft

Toby put a tack on Sister Nora's chair then confessed it to her after school

But Jimmy who hadn't seen his dad
In years was told by Father Frank
That he'd receive holy communion if he mouthed the holy scepter
and when he did he was told it was a sin to spit Jesus out

From that day forth Jimmy never doubted how bad he was

How She Grieved the Old Piano

The old upright should have been
undone with due reverence
screws backed out carefully
wires laid on carpeting
in the ascendancy of the notes they carried
woods musty with cellar dampness
--once given carefully selected veneers—
unhinged and set down softly
keys that offered *Clare de Lune* and *Pathetique*
— blacks and whites—extracted gently
albeit old now and out of tune

but my father demolished it with rude tools
crowbar and sledge hammer
as wood splintered and pedals loosed
and when the sounding board was finally separated from its cabinet
the mortally wounded instrument
groaned its last terrible note
as it smashed to the floor
on my mother's foot

it wasn't so much the hitch in her step I noticed after that
as her off key humming had ceased
and I saw this violence had created a hard place in their marriage
that never got back to tenderness

so after my father passed --as men usually do first--
she found a recording of Vivaldi's *The Four Seasons*
and played it often the rest of her winter years

The Way Station

You can hear it call around 4 a.m.
and if the wind driven rain crackles hard against the windshield
if it shakes the ground as it nears
if the crossing gates descend
with lights flashing as the warning bell clangs
as it heads north
because it always heads north
then you know it has come for someone
as age has ransacked another life

there will be news of it tomorrow
in this little town of no consequence
that someone has gone
far beyond the habitation of others
where night is just a bruise behind moon and stars
and there will be a vast stillness in this place
of forbidding cold until the wind has its say
until it brings the voices of all those known

and maybe this is only a way station
until another return to life

and the length of their days
Is now a squalid dream of toil and futility
except for the love given
except for that

The Migratory Habits of Dreams in Late Autumn

During the first cycle you may visit your childhood home
and they will all be there as though still alive
and there may be steaming pots
on the stove and your mother will turn to you and smile
and you will sit in a chair too big for you
while your dog settles his head in your lap

during your second cycle you dream of leaves
that have loosed themselves and drift and tumble
in quiet descent and with each you
give them the names of those who have passed
and whisper sweet prayers as your rake
gathers great drifts of them to a burn pile,
their smoky incense carried up to intersect
with a flock of birds

and in the final cycle
your breathing will slow and lengthen
as your breast heaves and settles
again ever slower and someone will read to you
as you feel the press of their weight on the bed
they will read soft words from a children's book
word by word by word
and pages will rustle like leaves
and there will be no need of anything
—all is said and done—
and you will be loosed
to rise and fall at the same time
as the earth recedes
you drift higher and are carried South
while a snow accumulates and whitens
everything below

Sunrise Suite for Cello and Piano

The music plays in my head as the bow draws a long note punctuated
by the piano keys.

There is little chance of survival now.

The sun emerges indifferently
to preside over the poisoned clouds
rising up like tall buttes.

Unholy rivers of traffic send their
messages into the sky.
You were not shed of man soon enough.

I ask myself do the birds know:
the egrets, the heron, the gulls that choke the sky
the gulls who will thin out when the silvery fish are gone?"

Does this baby know
held by his father
watching the terrible beauty of this dawn?

And somewhere in all of this
didn't we know it would come,
this slow motion apocalypse?
How can we not have seen all these fires
burning
and do nothing
except to console ourselves
by buying
eco friendly laundry soap
and saying "yes I talk the talk?"

We bequeath you now to the rats and roaches
who may very well be better stewards.

And to whom do i say
I am sorry?

Future Tense

There is a scrambling of the time continuum in this house
I hear the future occupants
—a young couple— working out their differences
I am haunted by their bumping and clanging
the way they pass through my corporal being
the way they fast forward me out of existence
upending my proprietary dwelling to theirs
I have fought mightily not to have my future visited upon me
and yet…

and then there are these demonic little savages
they claim as their children
with their insipid names
—Cassandra and Jonah—
crashing about my place
endangering me with their clutter
threatening to send me ass over tea kettle
with a misplaced creation" of plastic blocks

did I mention their hideous decor?
broken down couches and mismatched chairs.
badly rendered artwork (no doubt the children's)
taped to walls and the refrigerator
and my things are nowhere to be found

you should wake up some morning to find
you've been erased from your own home of 40 years

finally my late wife Maggie comes and extends a hand
"Come dear, "she says,
"It's time to go,"
so I shuffle along with her
because I've missed her more than I ever realized
and it wasn't a home without her anyway.

Night Train to Paris

Our aged bodies
surrender to the sway
and lurch of the train
as we have passed through
the long tunnel
beneath the sea

old is a foreign country
we ride to

when we get there
we will rise to higher places
sit with gargoyles
balance on slate roofs
as light slips through us
we sleep on park benches
dry leaves chasing around
us like wicked urchins

I will fish the river
in a floppy hat
mouthing a Gauloises
and you with a book splayed
in your lap will feed pigeons the remains
of your bread while sitting
on a soft blanket
and we will glance at each other
as only such longtime companions can with a pure knowing

later we will write postcards
from an empty bistro
—trumpet notes weave into the cool dark air—
telling the children back home

we are here now
and they will not see us again

Dmitri I Have No Music for This

How did you find the notes Dmitri
amongst artillery shells or the snare of machine gun fire?
I hear there were frozen corpses in the streets
and nowhere to bury them
while some ate wallpaper paste for lack of food
and when the Stukas screamed down
did you hear the minor chords
and convert them to a melody
for the violins and cellos
for your city who gathered the
starving to hear a starving orchestra
play your creation
while still surrounded

Dmitri I have no music for this
with the whole of mankind besieged
when even the ones you love
may carry the enemy
that will cull the old and the weak
when even a warm embrace is insidious
and we are turned against our own hands

Dmitri I have no music for this
when the hospitals are jammed to bursting
I only hear the congested wheeze
and the fevered delirium
when I look from the window and wonder
if the planet has turned irreparably
and will not turn back

Dmitri I have no music for this

(Dmitri Shostakovich wrote the Seventh Sympathy while Stalingrad was
under siege by the German Army during the Second World War.)

Ghosting

The aircraft lights wink behind the copse
of dying ash in the moments shy of dawn
soon the trees will tumble down
one and then another
to give a little more horizon
and who could know in the plane
that somewhere in their distance I watch

I have walked the long night
on the road by the sea
where lights are all that define the ships
plying the phosphorescent waves
but I don't know why

and I don't know how I became this…
at first I thought it was just a dreaming
or light headedness
but maybe I am
little more than a slip of smoke
from a guttered candle taken on a current of air
its afterimage held in the memories of a few

that my footfalls make no sound now…
that you passed me in the hallway this evening
and took no notice…

…and yet I follow a silvering of light
escaping beneath the bedroom door
(you have assumed some of my side of the bed now)
as I have come to remember
you are still my destination
and maybe you will lift your head
and say my name

Here I Sing

There you were Phillippe walking between two buildings
100 stories above the asphalt
on full display
a figurine to the crowd below
you only needed one misstep
one gust of wind to tilt you off that cable
—you and your balance pole—
snatched by gravity the way you'd always imagined it
nothing to catch you
they will turn away
or look horrified
as the pavement reaches for you and smashes you
your final seconds reflected in plate glass windows

so what if my voice skids off the notes?
will I feel gravity reach out for me?

Phillippe show me how not to fall
as I sing this next song
and climb the notes to the very edge of my range

did I tell you my brother broke his neck one morning just getting out of bed

so I ask you what am I doing

I am a soloist
I sing acapella
I balance on the high notes

the air is thin and my octave is a mile up
I get vertigo in these registers
how did you manage Phillippe
I might freeze in the spotlight
succumb to these eyes trained on me

I might sour a note and give myself to the tug of the earth
and all the rest of the day I'll return to that moment and die again

(On August 7, 1974 Phillippe Petit walked eight times between the World Trade
Centers balanced on a cable.)

Places I Have Known

Of this place
I wish to remember everything
the green out-cropped islands
left to wildness
stony ruins jutting over the thin division
of land and sky
with light diffused in gathered clouds
from a low sun

Hamlets less claimed by civilization
 the inflection of words;
and the staccato of foreign tongues
in teeming streets;
bridges trolled by the unwashed
for another coin in their cup

We still hear the music rise
to our open window in the night
to carry away our sleep
as we unravel a mournful dirge
from this land's brutal past

of you my love
I know vast tracks
I've known your taste
when need was everything
the slope of your shoulder
and the measure of your taken hand
the uptilt of your chin
just before you speak
and the topography
of your ear as you tuck a wisp of hair behind it

yet I may catch you
in an unguarded moment
after clearing dinner plates
and I can see the wine
has carried you
to archipelagos of darker thought

that are foreign to me where
I dare not take
my clumsy step
so I touch your cheek
and then you flash a smile
to say you've returned

Rain to Snow

As I surrounded your graying face
in my hands to say farewell
I looked up to see the rain
convert itself to snow
as if to validate your passing

homebound from the hospice
I skidded into a ditch
and pounded the steering wheel
shouting to no one
"Wasn't it enough that I lost my brother?"

waiting to be towed
soft accumulations of
flakes bore me to a muted
darkness and
I came to understand that you my brother
never stood a chance with father

everything to you was Herculean
eventually you broke
for lack of his softer words
and instead you chased his approval
even in the decades after he died

yet father told me years ago
how he admired you for all you'd done
so maybe you were loved
in some flawed way by him after all

and maybe there is no chance of purity
so much of love gotten or given
is refracted like a sunset wounding the sky
is kept in a reticence
is suffocated in parsimony
leaving us with our hungry places

Re-imagining My Father

I hear my mother's weeping
inside my voice

Some days it catches me up mid-sentence
and I cock an ear to its rasping protests

Her torn little phrases spit out
on gusts of emotion

and in some firing of memory
I see a boy in bed not sleeping

who was thinking about his birthday
the next day

until his father accused her
of being with another

Was this some crooked version
of love?

...his intense need of her?

and why do I want to rephrase this for him
so many years later

so he says something softer like:

"I'm so afraid of losing you
to someone else.
Please don't ever leave me."

Remembering Your Repeated Attempts at Living

Looking back now
you should have been admired
for dodging cars in downtown traffic
wishing to be broken
against chrome and steel

...congratulated for
confessing to the cashier
at the drugstore
that you were in a
state of grievous sin
(though your transgressions
could have only been slight)...

...applauded for trying
to jump from a moving automobile,
opening the door to a press
of air and blur of pavement,
because the world spun
too fast for you

...and cheered when you shuffled the halls
of the psychiatric unit
nearly insensible from thorazine...

But no one heard the
desperate eloquence
of your gestures, your attempts

Life blessed you
with its curses
and by the time
you mouthed the shotgun
that burst your eyes from their sockets
those eyes weren't seeing much
anymore anyway...

or maybe they were
looking toward
your next incarnation

Some Still Come to Ask

I should have been a student of the sky
to watch squadrons of geese make passage
beneath low autumn clouds.
Stars could lift my heart as I hold forth with
astronomical terms like "nebula" or "quasar"
and,
while in a hammock,
held in broad trees, I'll know
branches are emissaries
to other realms,
where the moons overpower reason.

I could acquaint myself
with the retired
who fish along the quay
and see their days in total
and find their peace
in the lap and lull of the water,
speaking just to quietly ask
"Are they biting today?"

I should have studied
 the nomenclature of the old
and listened to their lamentations
--- bad hearts and sad memories --
just to know that some still come to ask,
"Was this not heaven?"

TEN CENTS

Once
I saw a man,
whose brother
had been murdered,
sidearm a coin
into a fountain
and for years
I puzzled
over what this meant.

In the time
that followed
was the cheap prattle,
of weather speculations,
and baseball scores,
while his heartbeat kept time to some
inner dirge
that held him at a remove
and his countenance only broke once –
as he sailed the life of his brother
on a dime
into the water.

The Northern Lights

I never took your last breath;
you never saw my first.
So when I was young
I invented fathers
to take your place,
television dads
doting dispensers of wisdom
smelling of aftershave
and martinis.
I refused to learn to ride a bike,
certain you'd come along eventually
and teach me how.
Other times you shadowed me,
unable to reveal yourself
due to secret government work
but you'd save me in some moment of peril
at the last second,
only to vanish again.

By high school
Norman Rockwell was the cruelest man I knew
with all his paintings of normal.
and I hated everyone
who went on about how stupid their father was
"Try not having one," I'd think.

Finally when I was sixty
I bought an old truck
and drove deep into Canada
where I knew you last were.
It broke down twice
but, even though I could never fix
my bad marriages, I could fix trucks.

I was not ready
for the aurora
to back light the cemetery
where I stumbled around
and found your untended stone.

64

I was three beers into my night
and about to read a letter I wrote to you
where every sentence began with "why"
when something in me just let go
and I quietly whispered
"thank you dad"
and turned back to leave it all behind.

2 a.m. Charlie

There is a mouse that comes to my room in the black hours
I call him *2 a.m. Charlie*
I see his leavings peppering the corners

These nights remembrances play against the darkness of this long cold
season as though it were a movie screen

I am sorry for so many things now
For the widow down the road
For those in the path of armies
For how I treated you so long ago now
Do we only get it right when we are old

no trap can seem to catch him
much like memories that slip the snare

I stomp the floor and shout
"Go away Charlie"
He only quiets for a moment
Then continues about his skittering

The next night I think he comes with his family
And wakes me to
A greater panorama of thoughts
Go away Charlie
Please go away

Found

My father would lose his way in the city of Angels
in the tangle of freeways and unknown streets
with no one to call him *friend*
and tell him he would find his way

They say we should live in the moment
yet I get lost in the wilderness of my thoughts and the moment is gone

So I dreamed of the desert
finding myself in its blistering expanse
where I took my coordinates off the saguaro and the Joshua tree
I pitched my walking stick into a fire
offered my blood to the parched ground and sat and waited
even as the fear deepened in my bowels

this *time* I'd been given cycling down like a lengthening shadow

coyotes take my viscera and sinew take all my broken parts

And in this dream the hot Santa Annas
carried me across the sands
into the Gulf Stream into the jet stream
to the fire in the sky

I was way too old to be kept anymore
as I found my way back from all this separateness

West With the Night

You may have noticed me
hitching a ride with Beryl Markham
in a fragile biplane
—little more than a box kite with an engine—
while I sang *Waltzing Matilda*
to disguise my fear as wind gusts wobbled the craft
I could have had a tug of brandy
but I didn't want to miss how the land rushed away from us
as Beryl banked into a turn and set our course
while we bumped along in and out of the clouds
and finally the plane itself met its shadow
as we were jostled to a halt along the welcoming grasses

We had been somewhere over the Serengeti
or passing Kilimanjaro in the thin cold air
fighting off the press of downdrafts
as it struggled to overrule gravity
and simplify the world from a mile above

I am on the short end of my days now
and I should like one more ride before I evaporate into the night
before I become thin as moonlight
and dissolve in the memories of those who came after me
Beryl and I endlessly wandering the sky like gypsies

Every Single Toe

When you were old and thin and brittle
and could no longer reach your feet
I held them gently to trim your nails

I saw you next in your desperate hours
and wanted to travel with your thoughts
on those last and lonely days
did you go to your girlhood
or recall your first sight of dad
or remember the four babies you pushed out
and held
and held
but by then you were so far away
and the sheet that covered you
only registered the uneven rise and fall of your breath

so I oiled my hands and ministered to your heels
and arches
and to every single toe
and sang
hard times, hard times,
come again no more
all your miles behind you now
your breathing nearly gone

Gone Askew

The dawn was slumped over in a slop of gray
tearing the tops off of the waves.
This is where the sun should be.

The geese rise up in a discordant song while
the wind marks my face with its icy rain.
This is where the stars once dwelled.

I know you will not return today
I am a storm tossed vagabond set in small relief
against a setting orange moon
smudged with clouds.

This is where I should be.

Oh Ferdinand

Take me to your new world
I have searched the seedy taverns in their dim amber light
amongst a thin scattering of hopefuls
with the thumping blare of music

take me with your eyes
your lips
your hands
I will plant my flag

and we will circumnavigate our hungry bodies in one another's arms
invade with fingers and tongues
only to move on to other lands
half forgotten in the years to come
my name lost to you
your face gone from my memory

O Ferdinand did you have such hollow places too
did you substitute conquest for love
where will you go when all the lands are claimed
you and I both lost and bereft
our best days squandered
sharing our sad adventures
on a park bench
don't we make a fine pair
you in your ruffled cowl around your neck
and your pantaloons
examining the wreckage of one of your galleons
wondering
if you want too much do you always get too little

yet was there not one who caught your eye and stood you still

oh Ferdinand I once had a close brush with love too

Where We Left Off

Once I knew you like I know the journey of the winter's moon
behind a snare of branches
that I follow in my sleepless hours

once I knew you like I know the sun when it lifts to the horizon
and how it revealed our discontent

you spoke of my forays into the unlit passages of the soul
…and how that made you feel alone

so this is where we left off
and I have searched for your whereabouts
these many years later
just to pass on a gentle word
and let you know I have defeated some of that darkness
and only wish to bridge the terrible separateness I still feel
as I remember the times we use to dance to a long slow melody only we
could hear
shedding our defenses little by little

but time has had its way with us and in time I found you at your last
known address…
an unkempt cemetery on the edge of this little town where I still live

The Taggers

I have made my claim
tagging the alleyways
with red spray paint
and you who I never knew
signed your name on a subway car I rode one day

someone told me to let the wind and the rain pass through me
but I had to let them know I was here

famous men who stink of rotted meat insist on pressing
the Bible in my hands
and tell me lies they think I wish to know

while all day long planes scribble in the sky
and feed us their dirty air

yet every now and then
I see your name on a swaying boxcar
Chicago bound
my sweet brother *Reggie*
—letters in blue and orange and green—
your name is a work of art
you are not alone

Night Forest

Once there was a woman in the night forest
who could hear above the register of most.
She would listen to mice sing in chorus
or coyotes comfort their young
over the flash and rumble of coming weather.

There was the night when I stayed in the garden
late into the hours and you called for me
and together we watched the gods
toss stars across the sky and later
we returned to our bed and I watched you
over the vastness of our pillows
as your breathing fell into a rhythm
and you separated from me.

Have your dreams returned you to a wooded place,
dusted in moonlight, where you keen your ears
to other selves, selves beyond the register of my knowing?

I wish to thank my dear friend Sue Knauer for her reading of my poems and her honest commentary.

Thank you poet Ed Ruzicka for all your kind words and all our years of friendship.

Finally, thank you to Hank Stanton for all his encouragement, his fairness, and his generosity in giving me the opportunity to publish again and again.

Gary Beaumier is the author of two books of poetry *From My Family to Yours* published through Finishing Line Press and *Dented Brown Fedora* published by Uncollected Press. He has been a boat builder, a teacher, a garbage man, a bookstore manager and a gandydancer amongst many other occupations. He once taught poetry in a women's prison.

Meet Gary Beaumier! Gary is one of our 2023 Poetry Masters and one of our most beloved MATTER finalists. His poetry is featured across all three MATTER volumes; he's been blessing us with his high-caliber storytelling for years. He writes with a wistful, haunting tone that grabs a hold of you and pulls you out of your seat directly into a memory, evoking the exact same feelings Gary felt at that moment; and you feel them deeper than you ever thought possible. Gary is a great MATTER Poetry Contest success story. Team Oprelle would have never been able to promote his gripping poetry if it hadn't been for his thoughtful submissions.

Gary Beaumier has worked a vast array of jobs including teacher, bookstore manager, gandydancer and garbage man.
Over the past four years, he has won five writing contests for his poems including *Night Train to Paris*, *Sirocco*, *The Shape of My Absence* and most recently the Emily Dickinson prize for his poem *Spirit Animal*. His poem *Night Forest* won the Love Poetry contest, was nominated for a Pushcart Prize and is the title poem for a recently released anthology. His two books, *Dented Brown Fedora* and *From My Family to Yours* are through **UnCollected Press** and **Finishing Line Press**. He is a recent winner for his upcoming book of poetry *Tales of the Afterlife* that will be published by **UnCollected Press** later this year.

Gary Beaumier's writing is the type that keeps you thinking about it for days after you turn the page. Keep an eye out for his personal collection in our upcoming 2023 Poetry Masters Anthology: Coming soon.

Gary Beaumier's poems present crystal clear but novel new images - images that are so refined and honed they feel like long-absent and newly discovered friends - instantly recognizable and welcomed with amazement and love. The poems are a beautiful, soft flow of line and language emerging like a rill discovered in the obscurity of some literary, linguistic woodland. This is deeply compassionate and emotional poetry that never-the-less eschews sentimentality.

Henry Stanton,
Publisher, *Uncollected Press*

The poet manages to bare his soul in the perfect distillation of words - this is the work of Gary Beaumier. Raw, heartfelt, and aching with all the messiness and longing of life.

Mary Boyle
Managing Editor of *Ozaukee Living Local*

In these poems present, past, and even future coexist, death and life two sides of a coin. Beaumier deftly conjures--and honors--memory as a landscape where endless discovery beckons, where sanctuary may be found.

Virginia Small
Poet & Author of *Great Gardens of the Berkshires*

www.ingramcontent.com/pod-product-compliance
Lightning Source LLC
Chambersburg PA
CBHW020313090426
42735CB00009B/1323